To Jocelyn.
With best wishes.
Alan.

To Rocamadour

Other poetry by the author

The Green Tide (Rivelin Press, 1975)

To Rocamadour
and
other poems

ALAN HILL

RED BECK PRESS

2005

To Rocamadour is published by
Redbeck Press, 24 Aireville Road,
Frizinghall,Bradford BD9 4HH.

Typeset by Kath Leaver
67 Moorhead Crescent, Moorhead,
Shipley, West Yorkshire BD18 4LQ.
Telephone: 07976 950 447

Design and print by Tony Ward,
Arc & Throstle Press, Nanholme Mill,
Shaw Wood Road, Todmorden,
Lancashire OL14 6DA.

To Rocamadour
ISBN 1-904338-09-7

Redbeck Press acknowledges financial
assistance from The Arts Council England,
Yorkshire.

Acknowledgements
Five poems, *From the Bishop's Road, At Downhill Castle, At Drumcliff (1960), On Ilkley Moor* and *On Ilkley Moor at Corpus Christi* are reprinted from Alan Hill's earlier volume *The Green Tide* (Rivelin Press, 1975). *On Ilkley Moor* first appeared in *Phoenix.*
The quotation which appears in *Family Tree* (p.56) is an adaptation of a detail in Bede's account of the conversion of Edwin of Northumbria, quoted in Michael Alexander's *The Earliest English Poems* (p.64) Penguin Books, 1966.

To my wife Nan,
the other half of “we”
in most of these poems

Contents

ILKLEY
&
IRELAND

Tutorial

Kindly, but concerned.
with even voice I ask about her work.
So much behind – what's done is very good,
but thinly spread. The flavour isn't – strong.
My gently smiled regret is met
by her own smile of compassion
for my evident pain.

So, quietly, she tells me why her work
has not been done. And in the room
the silence extends like a still pond
now smoothly rippled by her careful words,
which fall blandly like eye-drops with no sting
until the sight is blurred.
                    And the priestly stillness
heard her confession of her father's fault,
her mother's despair, her own involvement
in the legal proceedings, and her fear
for her brother and sisters
abandoned and unsupported.

I heard the report,
listening gravely with adjusted face,
and felt amazement as the windows shook
and the building quaked, but with no sound.
And my hand which wanted to reach out and catch her
remained on my lap, composed, *comme il faut*,
as she fell from my sight
into her life.

Morris Men at Broadway. 1953

All those years ago, in summer,
we wandered in the cool night air,
breathing the heavy scent of hay-fields
and the damp odour of old walls.

Then music on the still air
gathered us, like bees to clover –
pale faces in the dusk
cordoned round the Morris Men
in the dark inn yard.

Woven patterns of white shirts,
coloured scrolls of ribbons streaming,
jig of knee-bells and legs stamping
in a language like the sound of summer rain.
They stepped in stately gaiety,
not solemn but unsmilingly,
as if they wrote upon the ground
in newly-mastered characters of sound
and patterns measured in their bounding.
They danced as if their music's treading
jolted up the grass again
and moved the planet round.

And at their close,
when they were men again,
their bells put by,
still loth to move,
we lingered,
like moths after a lamp has been extinguished.

A Winter's Tale

She said, "How romantic of Shakespeare, in the end
to let a shepherdess marry a prince."
But Perdita was a princess all the time,
so Florizel was assured of his father's blessing.

Which always strikes me as closely resembling
that masterstroke of the merchandiser's subtle art
of permitting us to purchase at a great reduction
a half-weight packet in a double size.

Autolycus put his finger on the same button
by remaining faithful and deceiving his king.
In *Measure for Measure* Will did it again,
marrying a hypocrite to a virtuous wife
who faithfully deceived him by losing her virginity.

A pox on such paradox. I prefer Brutus
who nobly assassinated his friend and benefactor
with the best of intentions, but got the chop.

In December

(Tanka 15)

The advancing dark,
like a progressive disease,
lingers more each day;
grows bolder with each attack,
and goes more slowly away.

Askwith Lane

That oak wears an ivy jacket;
the other sunlit-silver trees
bear their patinas of green moss,
bright as slime on a summer pond.

A little bird skims a hedge-top –
wren or sparrow I cannot tell –
quick as a moving patch of light,
unconscious of mortality.

Cows in roughened coats stand in clouds
of their own winter's-morning breath,
four still feet planted, smelling sweet,
passively unaware of death.

Past the house like Dove Cottage
the car swings in the deep lane;
the Wordsworths and Coleridge –
imagination and pain.

Near Armagh

(Tanka 20)

With a heavy stick
I killed a myxy rabbit.
Three blows only broke
its back, the fourth its neck, and
my taste for intervention.

Lilies of the Valley

Have you seen thistles bursting through tarmac,
breaking their bonds, like Gulliver yawning?
If any, then these spiky survivors
would be the ones to do it, you might think.
If our ears were capable of tuning
to their pitch, we should hear their triumphant roars.

But what sound when lilies of the valley
spear their straight ways like driven bayonets
through this (as we thought) life-smothering crust?
Slender shoots, smooth as petals of poppy,
but, protected by their bronzy sleekness,
they are tough as women, and breathe sweet musk.

Tanka 40

Look how the sunlight,
glittering off the water,
wavers on the reeds,
mimicking the dragonflies
in quivering flakes of light.

Woman by the River

By the river you passed, and stared to see me
standing alone, eating a sandwich,
fixedly watching the brown water
swirling in eddies round that fallen tree.

Must I, because I am solitary, hide?
Is my lone figure on the river path,
where the ramblers pass and the couples glide,
blasphemy against the spring – a whiff of death?

You observed my stockings, my brown tweed,
my glasses, grey hair – all my scars of age.
Oh I know my appearance well; indeed
I understand your hastily averted gaze.

If I am lonely it is my own fault,
for I cannot seize the idle word,
bend and hammer it into conversation.
Words are not currency for me,
but brittle, unsure bridges where
I dare not trust my weight to cross
that black silent chasm between us.

Yes, I am a spinster. But I like the smell
of newly laundered curtains in my room.
I have my pleasures –
hyacinths are almost a passion with me –
Oh, four, sometimes five big bowls, china bowls
I plant, and watch them as they grow each year.

You did not speak. (The dirty always speak.)
Yet a word might have proved me visible;
though my throat's closure, or tongue stuck
would have left me staring, inaudible.

No matter. Lulled by the river's eddies,
I can remember, as a child,
our walks by the river at home,
and Uncle John, so different from my father,
swinging me up on to his shoulder,
and singing as we swayed along.

Commedia

The other day I heard of a father
who wouldn't continue to support his daughter
because she wanted to marry her lover
before her college course was over.

Another girl embraced the Roman religion
in order to take the marriage communion,
despite her father's violent opposition.
She too was beggared in a brutal fashion.

Reflecting on this sad half-comedy
with no Arlecchino to provide a remedy,
I wonder on what irrelevant absurdity
my children may provoke my Pantaloon rapacity.

From the Bishop's Road

(Avish, Co. Londonderry)

From the Bishop's Road
you look down on the backs of seagulls and rooks
hung like mobiles beneath you,
too high for shadows to fleck the fields below them.
From this flying height
the coloured map of land lies spread like history.
Dark trees conceal the roads that string the square farms,
but the sun's keen eye
glints on the iron rails of the Derry line
which sunders farm from fields
and cows from byres.
And the rails have made remote
the English tower that stands on the yellow Point
besieged by sand-dunes like forgotten peasantry.

Above the Lough's bright water, where the white tide foams,
mist-blue Inishowen sprawls
like a coal-measure, waiting for the world's sunlight.
On the yellow strand, where the Lough funnels seaward,
a reef of sea-shells –
sea-life's refuse scattered by tides and wheeling birds –
present brown faces,
white-ribbed and hollow sockets,
to the crushing sand and steps of wandering men.
The sea's past rattles to the land's present, passing;
the past, unburied, dissolves into the present.

Down at the cliff's foot
the wind ripples the green tide of the meadow grasses
and slow cloud shadows move
like lazy creatures gliding through a green sea's depth.
There by the field's edge, wrecked, by the hedgerow,
a motor car corrodes into rust
like brown foil that trembles as the wind shakes it;
like the past's other refuse it lies unburied.
I saw a broken charnel-house in Kerry once,
unfenced except by nettles, and guarded by cows,

and a wealth of scattered bones was all its treasure.
Here the unburied ones shake in the bare branches
like ash-keys in March.

On Ballywalter Strand

Two men stepping along the strand,
mounting briefly the grey spurs of rock
that poke like bones through ancient skin
and point, like fingers, from the land

to where the mist stretches from the bay's tip
across the sea, greyly gauzing
the distant lighthouse, and displacing
the repeating fog-horn, like sounds in sleep.

The two men talking as they tread the strand,
one young, one old, the elder telling how
he holidayed in haylofts forty years ago.
But then they cross a name scratched in the sand –

only the name – *Adèle* – and the sound
of the insistent fog-horn, a lighthouse,
and two men walking into the mist
towards the tide, on Ballywalter Strand.

At Downhill Castle

(Built by the Bishop of Londonderry c.1770)

In a cornfield, where wheat grows up to the windows,
Downhill Castle stands blind-eyed and bleak in the wind
that shakes and rustles the bending stalks around it;
stands and is falling.
Behind its Gothic ramparts whose gates sag open
in courtyard and in stables and through salon walls
the nettles grow green and tall to the small, square sky.
The mitre and the white bands have not survived here,
but the benevolence of the episcopal hands
establishing decorum from barren thistles
lingers, derided by this mocking barbican's
Gothic gesture, standing dark against the green tide
of wheat shaken by the wind.
Evening strollers scramble, calling quietly
to beware a broken stair.
Limp barbed wire sways slightly in the cooling air.

From the falling gates
a fenced, precise, narrow path aims through the tall wheat
down a gentle slope to where, on a mown greensward,
a small round domed building rests elegant, weightless
– nicely balanced like the doctrine of Trinity
  and similarly stranded by the tide of time –
above the sickening cliff that rises from the
long, slow, creeping lines of foam on the sea below.
My Lord Bishop's library, preserved intact
in spite of the ravages of war and weather.
Oblivious of time it stands there, serene
in the slight evening air,
alone and clear,
perfect as a cockle shell
on an empty strand.
Quiet holidaymakers stand in its shade
tranquil and easy, gazing at the wide prospect,
the Bishop's heirs, by time's deeds.

At Drumcliff 1960

Under Ben Bulben
        and these clouds that glide all day
from the Atlantic
        across the wind-washed sky,
Drumcliff's grey tower
        lifts its pinnacle fingers
in a foreign pride,
        and its low door swings slightly
in the bright sea-wind.

Under the dark raftered roof
        where whitewash flakes off
and damp dissolves the plaster,
        the gentry moulder –
remote from this place as those
        for whom the turquoise
peacock's cries under the trees
        palled to gaudy shrieks –
with the emperors, their courts,
        their golden fountains,
and all their sweet captived flesh
        joined in unceasing
processions which continue
        to be forgotten.

Now the gentle air disturbs
        the lazy motes that
hang in the latticed sun-shafts.
        Here is no sound
but the petulant mutter
        of the grumbling hens
who lift their feet at the door
        but do not enter,
discontentedly pecking
        in the clouds' shadows
scarcely seven feet from where
        unseen beneath turf
the remains of Yeats are laid.

Imperturbably
        the hens scrape and peck round this
dead volcano's edge;
        the pipe is stopped and cold, but
the fires still burn
        under this sleeping island;
dreamers moan and turn
        beneath the grass, and above,
where brown hens mutter
        and cast a cold eye on life,
on death, and pass by
        the gate where a celtic cross
stares over hedges
        where torn linen heaving like
a woman's sobbing
        blows itself dry in the wind
that all day long drives
        the clouds' shadows like cattle
up Ben Bulben's slope.

Letter to Lima

(For D.J.T. 1970)

Now, like second sons
we fill no paternal hearths,
but like landless men
seek our fortunes here or there,

like seabirds, crying
across the waste of ocean,
calling, to recall a
memory of dry land.

Words now from my tongue,
hard, like half-remembered runes,
rise but half bidden
to a work half understood,

released from the stone
carved by man and wind and rain,
their virtue not known,
then sink like water in sand.

But by words to stand –
stand against the world's turning.
We, men with no land
make no harvest or planting.

Only the high words
we let fall on unploughed earth
like thistledown seed
born on air, from stone brought forth,

they can thrust bursting
through the world's black tarmac crust
like lust in a bank,
pound notes and pin-stripes burning.

Word. Only the word
snatched away by the rude wind,
petals on ruins,
chance-grown wallflower, ragwort

gay yellow and bright
or soft russet sweet-scented
on ruined walls rooted.
But on this March night

In wind-swept Ilkley
these words stumble from my tongue
to sing, though vainly,
uncrowned dynasties unsung.

Senryu

Spring blossoms in May.
Birds busy collecting twigs.
Men looking for work.

On Ilkley Moor

Beside the path to Heber's Ghyll
stands a grey stone, squared and upright.
It is weathered roughly smooth like the others,
and I would have passed it by, had Kate
not pointed out the writing as she scampered by.

But I, with my fingers, traced the letters,
worn now by eighty-five years of rain
from the north-west which it faces up the Dale.
Neat and squarely carved, the letters
must have been made with hammer and chisel
and conscious art.
Two inches high, they record four names,
a date, a place, and one word now dissolved.

And as my fingers traced the lines
guessing the curves and the raised holes,
I wondered at your ancient adventure,
not very daring, up from Cleckheaton,
on the ladies' path, not the Moor proper,
boaters and flannels, unsoiled probably,
tea in the town and the band by the river
before you caught the train for Bradford,
and back to Monday morning on the tram.

But you came, whether for a bucko's frolic
or to breathe and open your town-scaled eyes
I can't tell; but the squareness,
the lapidary firmness of your letters
and your chosen tablet facing up the valley
make me glad that today I learned of
W.E. Hicks *H. Wilson*
S. Chapman *F. Collins*
who, one day in eighteen eighty-three
deliberately chose this site for their monument
and jointly, like forgotten pharaohs,
made their stand against the rolling sun.

Three Insect Poems

1
Wood Lice

I like wood lice,
though at one time they made me shudder.
Grey and unaggressive,
they huddle together under rotting wood,
apparently for companionship,
or perhaps because they lack ambition
to leave the ancestral pile and seek their fortunes.

And have you seen them alarmed,
curling into little balls like folding marbles?
Armour-plated little nobodies,
but armoured against what?
Can their leathery backs protect them
from the stabbing of a bird's beak?
But perhaps they are proof against ant bites.

They aren't often flushed from their private covers,
but when a casual foot kicks the roof aside,
wood lice are like most of us who have not
the spider's speed nor the earwig's rakish pincers;
they duck their heads. But if the foot is bigger
than their little strength can stand,
they die; just like us.

2
Flies

For flies, who love dung and putrefaction,
suck men's and beasts' blood and perspiration,
and persecute the labour of mankind,
one consolation only can I find –
when Man, animals and vegetation
are dead, flies will be one rot behind!

3
Earwig

Now your earwig is an individualist;
you rarely see more than one at a time
except, to my knowledge, in plum trees,
and that is only when the plums are ripe.
With the regulation six legs,
and a shiny brown body like a polished riding-boot
he is a *pukka* insect, and he walks alone.
He does not fight unless he is threatened,
but then he will turn and raise his gallant pincers
against the ridiculous odds of a booted foot.
A tiny head with hardly any brain at all,
and two curved pincers to take one with him when he goes.

An Educational Publisher's Catalogue

A publisher's catalogue, archly reclining,
seductively slender, of elegant hue,
extends on my table, mischievously smiling,
permitting whatever I'm willing to do.

Its pages are parted, like soft lips, expectant,
inviting my fingers to open them more.
Some pages may make a pretence of reluctance,
exciting my hand to insist and explore.

At last it has yielded, awaiting our pleasure;
the questing is over – but passion's no more,
for lurking, revealed by the final exposure,
no virgin but – draining my lust – an old whore.

Tintagel

We didn't like Tintagel,
and we didn't see the castle
for we couldn't park the car
and the Whitsun crowds were dense
in the hot dusty streets.
And we didn't see Merlin's cave
for not all his magic could compel
those dull incurious eyes
to see anything but rock.

Of Mark the King there is nothing left,
but the Round Table lives on
reproduced in many gift shops,
while Lancelot is a guest-house,
and Guinevere a tea-shop.
So we left Tintagel quickly
and drove to a quieter place
where my daughter picked foxgloves,
as young Arthur might have done.

Crocodile

The sun is his friend,
scrubs his back, his only warmth.
The water his mother he lies on,
drifts in, eats in.
Big leather belly and jaws
borne up by the green water.
No alarms, unthreatened, unthinking,
no movement
until
to the water come to the drinking
the uneasy, the young and unwary,
the old and limping
then
sliding, gliding, homing on target
go the jaws, the eyes unwinking
with scarcely a ripple disturbing
the silent water
and
with a tail's swing
smash the legs off balance
and grab
drag
down
and drown
struggle and bite gripe

Sink and kick, and shuddering twitch.
Grow still, soft.
Then bite, tear, chomp,
wrench, roll and twist.
torn, the raw flesh on tooth, jaw.
Madden and swallow to fill
stop that one pain
that one blemish in the cool water
in the warm sun and the light.

Hide, muscle and gut in the sun
with ease and mastery of all
necessary manoeuvres fitted.

* * *

Your smooth skin, my dear,
and delicate fingers that stroke,
gentle eyes and wistful smiling lips
are meat to him.
But he's a handbag and shoes to you

* * *

The crocodiles that I fear
wear suits in strong checks,
comfortingly filled across the shoulders.
Their calves swell through worsted
as they stand braced and bouncing at a bar.
And they smile at you with cold eyes
when you make a joke they do not understand.

Aeroplane

Great-bellied bird on turbined wings
swing low over the land
over the buried bones and the fleshed ones
over the blackbird's song and the butcher's laughter
over the rotting canal and the blackened road.
Roar your tilted thrust up to the clouds
that drift and fall, in the unceasing sequence
that softly carves away the bedrocks of being.

Soar like the fluted trunk
of the rooted beech where the blackbird sang
looking this way and that to challenge intruders;
and I, blind in my human foolishness
lifted my heart to the imagined joy.
Rise like the voice of the butcher's boy
as the cleaver descends
smashing bone and tissue asunder
parting sinews, making parcels of flesh.
Lift as the boat in the lock lifts
inches above cans and bottles in the mud,
while the sliming gate restrains
the crash and tumble of the ducted waters.

Trace in soot from exhausted power
your course that cannot exceed a circle.
Ferry your varied cargo of chromosomes;
mingle and tangle into a skein
the chains of nucleic acids. Infect
and disperse the infected.
Bomb as with birdshit the disaffected
scatter like birdshot the propaganda
swoop as a hawk and tear the ungodly
of whatever creed profaned, and kill.

And make whole the dreams of those who believe
in your beauty of line, your grace of progress,
and believe, in the folly of their human hearts
that your summer's day distant ebbing drone
is a kindly sound like the blackbird's song
who shouts his fearful calls of defiance
from the beech tree or the lilac branch.

Motorway Construction at Castle Bromwich

The river, like a delved and dirty drain,
nudges the hillside back a bit each year;
and the castle mound, washed bare by the rain
dissolves slowly down into the river.

Above the river but below the mound
a red terrace contours the hillside
in a raw swath, and levels the broken ground
and hawthorns where we outlaws used to hide.

Along this motorway millions will go
unawares, across the slope where we rolled
shrieking with laughter in the sledging snow –
memories, buried now, like fairy gold.

For Sale

Here are new detached houses,
smart, coppery and sharp-edged
just like brand new bright pennies,
each rawly sliced from other
like blocks of red Cheshire cheese;
and the naked brickwork like
plain-stitch knitting inside-out.

Excellent propositions
for profitable re-sale
when Fortune throws a double
and moves you on twelve spaces.
But here you plant no fruit trees,
for current new pence tarnish
long before apples ripen.

Tanka 4

To please his friends, O
made himself into a drum,
silent until struck.
Thus he was not heard until
the army's march had begun.

Inside the Shell

(for Joyce Simpson)

As a young man I wore no armour,
and so moved quickly but was often wounded.
When my edge was blunted on an iron shell
I swore that old men had no feelings.

Now, slower and armoured, reluctant to riposte,
in age, I receive the young men's thrusts
and see them shrug, amazed at my unfeeling;
while I find that protected flesh still bruises.

Tanka 1

Shipwrecked leaf steers
to avoid a sucking drain.
Red hawthorn tears
drip along the sodden lane.
Autumn's drowning in the rain.

On Ilkley Moor at Corpus Christi

Today the Moor, under a warm haze,
softened by ferns and lulled by the sun,
seems to recline, and suffers the sheep
to crop among its tasselled grasses
like a nursing sow.
                                        Stonechat and lark
flit and hover, cursing and calling,
and the slender grasses thresh under the soft wind.

Lambs and children bleat at a distance,
and over the valley the grey haze,
warm, like a fallopian nimbus,
broods a thunder of vegetation
over the immemorial earth.

It is still, in spite of the darting birds
and the tremulous flicker of ferns;
still, as though waiting for the last change
of a long geological age.

Nothing happens, but stonechat and lark
flit between fern fronds, hover and swoop
into new generations of
blaeberry, heather and whin.
and delicate grasses, green and blue,
shake in an immemorial wind.

PERTHSHIRE

I wish we'd said goodbye

When the time came,
and we were really going,
and we couldn't
just drop in again tomorrow
to collect anything we'd left,
and there was no excuse for
not saying goodbye at last,
we made a point of saying
that we wouldn't say goodbye
because of course we'd meet again,
and very soon.

I wish we'd said goodbye,
and risked the tears
that would have shown
how much we loved and needed,
and how deep the chasm we were crossing,
and how unwise we were to go.
If we had said goodbye, little poem
you might never have been written.

Tanka 5

A politician
stands in bronze, erected by
a grateful empire.
For nothing, that I know of.
No wonder they were grateful.

The New Job
or
The Invisible Man

I am fading.
Definitely fading.

I am visible in corridors
for people smile at me and ask me how I am.
But in the office –
in the office I am fading.

The telephone calls are not for me.
I call others to the telephone,
and try to ignore their busy conversations
which remind me that no one
needs to talk to me about
anything important, apart from
how am I, and do I like it here?
But I do not say "No, because I am fading."

They must believe that what they see
is the real me,
who may be a Disappointment,
or a Puzzle,
but not *A Problem.*

A disappointment you can live with;
a puzzle you can solve;
but a problem you must do something about,
and I do not want anybody
to do something about me
for I might fade altogether
and become
dispensable.

In the South they call it Spring

(for Philip and Margaret Whidden)

Up here in March the undropped northern lambs
still swell the ewes' flanks.
Plovers tumble on the bullying wind
rolling and whistling,
figure-of-eighting to the muddy sheep,
indifferent still
to the giddy birds' sudden green and white
in the brief sunlight.

The rising curlew's liquid call proclaims
life on the bleached grass;
and snowdrops, and the winter aconite
are flowering now.

Black trees; sodden fields; sleet showers;
but birdsong, and flowers.

Tanka 43

"You are not," she said,
"the kind of man girls sleep with.
No!" she said, "You are
the kind they want to marry."
This news did not rejoice him.

Mole

Mole, unenlightened,
burrowing and circumscribed
by your tunnel's sides.
No need of vision
in those narrow spaces where
your flanks fit the walls,
a deliberate missile
reaming its own bore,
homing on worms to fuel its drive for
food and subterranean
reproductive will.

Flesh, fur, bone moving –
live gobbet in a delved gut –
mole crawling through earth.

Has no mole ever
in his warm snout-dug dark run
lusted for sunlight?
Inconceivable –
wonder no part of moleness.
Snout, belly and jaws,
and for travelling
under the recumbent earth,
two pink, spade-like paws.

The Suicide

His secret,
locked in his head
while he lived,
escaped unobserved
through the hole in his skull
when he died.

Tanka 3

Su Shih was banished
into a remote province,
where he lived and died
obscure. Too poor to travel,
he received the wild geese.

Generations

I am a watershed
drained and arid.
From my desert peak
time erodes
all the covering.
Even the bone
is scored and pitted.

Generations
before and behind
hang from me like ice that,
gathered on a sheep's fell,
tears the flesh finally
and bares the backbone.

I was a bowman
trained to the arrow
at a time of muskets.
I was practising
the parry of octave
when Hiroshima and Nagasaki.

Ghostly and unnoticed, I
thread a way to the drying pool
that will be dust before I reach it.
This private desert,
crossed by throngs of unnumbered young
who plant their green oases here,
is inhabited by me alone.

These worlds, like photographs superimposed,
co-exist in space and time.
They walk my sands and pick their flowers.
I fade from drought in their green bowers.
Two sides of a coin, we stay together,
but meet never.

The Silver Apples of the Moon

The golden apples of the sun
that cast no shadows, shine and burn –
prizes for the fit and striving,
lust for lustre, gust for gleaming.
Agents of delight love doing,
laughter and flesh, fragrant laurel,
leaping and lovely living on
the golden apples of the sun.

But loved by those who walk alone,
the silver apples of the moon
people with cool reflective light
the shadowed silences of night;
and make of vacancy a loom
for weaving fragments into dream,
and fabricate a living scene
from words half-heard, and truth part-known.

Vanellus Vanellus

Peewit, peesie, lapwing, plover,
looping, wheeling, diving over
moor and ploughland, grass and clover.

Plover, lapwing, peewit, peesie,
making aerobatics easy;
bird and spring day bright and breezy.

Peesie, peewit, plover, lapwing,
bright blue sky and white clouds dappling
fields with shadows, bush and sapling.

Lapwing, plover, peesie, peewit,
calling *Leave it! Leave it! Leave it!*
and I call again to tease it.

Peewit, peesie, lapwing, plover,
calls no more, and summer's over.

Ardoch Fort

(for D.J.T.)

One day in autumn,
with Tish and Michi and Patrick and Jane
you brought the warmth of fellowship and old friends;
and we were almost complete, except for Nan
who could not steal away from the thistle school
where she walked barefoot, hardening only slowly.

And the sun shone,
and we picked and poked over
the tumbled yard and the sagging byre
and the crumbling mill with the huge waterwheel
where the rats scampered at night,
and sometimes by day.

I had the pleasure of the knowing guide,
and you and the kids were like eager beagles
following scents and flushing secrets,
barking and yelping excitement and delight.
We went in procession through
the inquisitive village.
Net curtains twitched to our calling and laughter
as, after long parting we resumed
our talk and fellowship like musicians
tentatively playing unpractised
but long remembered tunes.

Through the gate and up the banking
I was waiting for the astonished cries
that I knew would rise when we breasted the crest
and you saw the extent of Ardoch Fort.

And we traced
the interleaved and mazing ditches
re-constructing the javelin shots
and ballista bolts that we conjectured
might be beneath our feet and the short grass

and the rabbit droppings and the tormentils.
And Patrick, grave and inspired,
telling how the Romans were armed,
how organised, and how they were dressed.

And hearing him, I saw two little boys,
one of them his father – do you remember?
– nearly forty years ago
discussing military tactics
in play, and in earnest too,
persecuted by rough boys who
were no doubt goaded by
our accents and differences.

. . . And I remembered the final battle,
when with overwhelming allied force
and cunningly prepared strategy,
we drove them howling from the Common,
running to their mothers.
And the unaccustomed exultation
of winning for once –
a strange flavour I have tasted since
when, with guile and infinite concentration
I have stalked a rabbit and shot it cleanly,
tinged with regret and a shaft of guilt
as then, so many years ago,
in that bitter guerrilla warfare
thrust upon us by the badge of class
that we carried, unawares;
– and that instinctive innocent ferocity
that finally we unleashed
upon them, our tormentors,
hounding them to their very doorsteps,
snivelling, snotty, abject . . .

* * *

And then the walk homeward, back to Silverton,
a straggling procession over the burn,
the bolting rabbit and the children's excitement,
and the contented calm of friendship
made flesh in hands and faces again
after the long but enduring link of letters
from the furthest places of the world.

* * *

That was three years ago.
And I was amused
to see you put on glasses for the drive south,
saddened too that age should mark you,
delving parallels,
and knowing yet another bond
of common kind between us –
as between all men –
but in us known and dwelt on,
as pace for pace, in one place or another,
time passes us through its workshop.

Tanka 21

Drifting clouds' shadows
darken but do not disturb
these quiet hill slopes;
so quiet you can almost
hear the slow Earth turning.

At Silverton

(Tanka 6)

The patter of rain
and the lick of the fire;
the cat flicks an ear;
the slowing globe spins time, which
passes quietly here.

Tanka 63

I came to Scotland,
and lost my way. But – praise the
gods of mist and peat –
I discovered whisky, and
at length, found a narrow path

Leaving Silverton

Come other springs,
and swallows will be here to welcome May,
swifts and martins nesting in the eaves,
and that thrush singing in the apple tree
will still sound gay.

Another spring
and who looks out will see the ancient land
coloured by the west wind and the plough,
and the high hollow where snow lies till May.
But I shall be away.

Next springtime,
and the endless wind scouring the wide sky,
the rolling plovers squealing all the day,
the mournful haunting curlew's call, will all
be memories.

EDINBURGH
&
IRELAND

Family Tree

My grandfather died in Ledsam Street –
collapsed on the pavement in thick fog,
walking home from the iron-foundry.
Sixty-eight, and died on the pavement;
his death an indisputable fact;
but his life? His sixty-eight years
of childhood, and food, and working and walking?
No more than reported rumours
now casually chanced upon, or lost,
according to the swing and smack
of bobbing conversational flotsam
sometimes on the surfaces
of his two surviving children's minds.

So like a beachcomber I sift for facts
through words, expressions, tones and pauses,
establishing no more than these:
Born in Stourbridge in eighteen sixty-eight,
and christened William John.
Several brothers and sisters, names forgotten.
Bouts of drinking punctuated
by abstemious bad temper.
By trade an iron bedstead maker,
once he was brought home by his mates,
a foot burned by molten iron –
six months off work, the family fed
by my grandmother taking in washing,
and my father delivering papers.
A trade-unionist, he was shop-steward,
and he always voted Conservative.
At twelve years old he walked to work,
seven miles with his father along the cut
and seven miles home, a hundred years ago.

Which is all that remains of a life –
No headstone, no portrait, no letters;

not even a family bible;
only an insignificant figure
standing, impassive, among sepia wedding guests.
The poor have scant memorials.

So I write these remnants of a life,
shadows of an obscurity;
for though "like swifts flying through a hall
we go from dark to dark through brief light,"
those slight sparks of memory that
recede fast into the past like tracer
mark the linear way with structure
like a kind of meaning. Neither statues
nor memorial tablets in parish churches
record my life's sources, generations past.
I grew like a thistledown seed
in a crack in a city pavement.
But a thing I know – a fact to root in –
my grandfather died in Ledsam Street.

Elegy I

I think I would prefer an Ulster funeral.
There they really know what death means, and treat it
familiarly, but with reverent decorum –
traditional turn-outs, black, bold and unashamed.
Ceremonially laid to rest in Roselawn –
suggestions of fragrance and trim tranquillity.
And attended only by relative strangers
mourning an image of vague credit and success,
status and probity untested by knowledge
of my many failures. And my coffin carried
by the younger menfolk, frowns lending dignity
and demonstrating grief – a hero's obsequies –
the women at home preparing refreshments. Yes,
I think I would prefer an Ulster funeral.

Elegy II

After the young bloom's beauty
and the pollen-ecstasy,
the shedding of the petals
and the ovary swelling.

Preoccupied with seeding,
the petals aren't regretted.
Secure in a green purpose
the shaped and graceful seed head
grows like an expanding smile.

But afterwards what remains?
Only to bleach and wither
in the pale autumn sun – a
dried husk shaken by the wind.

Elegy III

(Derek Langlois, d. 1988)

He emigrated in nineteen seventy-one,
because Australia offered a better life,
he said, an opportunity for man and wife
to make a stronger marriage, to begin again.

And then for seventeen years we corresponded,
long, yearly letters recounting our common rounds.
But his last broke off abruptly, and then I found
his wife's brief letter, telling me that he was dead.

That was two years ago; but I do not believe
the pain of that moment will ever be quite eased –
his ordinary, unique and known self deceased
without warning, and without having taken leave.
His feelings, sights and sounds, and all his thoughts have ceased.
I who live on, diminished by his death, still grieve.

Shakespeare Country

No tree left living of all those whose shade
might have enticed him or where he might have lain
for half a long summer's day alone
with the cuckoo's late call and the constant blackbirds;
or warm and close with a willing girl
with dusty feet and brown legs,
strong arms, and teeth, and appetite
– on a stolen Sunday or holiday –
firm and whole as the kernel of a good nut,
bonny and smiling through half-closed eyes.
Some Marian or Margaret or brown-haired Susan
who would crunch him like a pippin in an afternoon,
and for weeks after hum a little tune
when she remembered the tickle of the grass
and his permitted mastery.

No earthen crock or jar preserved
that might have poured him buttermilk, sour beer
or good ale of an evening.
No oaken trencher or sycamore bowl
for sopping bread, and withered apples;
all split and burned to warm some later evening
after he was dead.
No iron latch unrusted that he might have lifted
to seek the ease of gossip with a crony,
help a childhood friend or neighbour,
bring a stone of flour, borrow cloves,
or visit his relations –
overtly welcomed, silently appraised –
a visitation from remote places
tolerated on account of kinship,
but drinking their ale like any man,
and looking askance at little Betty's sores
just as the Parson's curate did.

Tam Faustus at Fifty

1

"Nothing to receive,
and nothing of worth to give.
Left only with the
overwhelming tedium
of continuing to live."

2

"I have prayed for death,
and my prayer has been answered,
but with irony.
Death has not stopped my body;
it has withered my spirit."

3

In Tam's carapace
a random brain cell flashes
faintly a girl's face,
like pale sunlight on far hills,
a distant glimpse of youth's grace.

4

Thirty years ago
he gave a silver locket,
a token of love.
He wonders if she kept it,
and why he should care to know.

5

There's no re-tracing
a path that has been severed.
Only memories,
like old wounds, sometimes aching,
according to the weather.

6

He stalks sedately,
Seeking still his Marguerite.
A schoolgirl lithely
swings her hips at a blond boy –
Tam's heart – misses a beat.

7

Young men and women
hand in hand with love brighten
The Royal Mile.
But all the swallows have gone,
though the sun shines a brief while.

8

Their bright eyes are bold,
for love draws a ring of gold
around them. But the
cold lust of a man grown old
could chill their brightness to dust.

9

"This wasting disease
of age makes me yearn for a
Mephistopheles
to conjure for me smooth hips,
and warm, fervid, eager lips."

10

"Now, before the snow
of whining age for ever
chills my passion – Oh
Come! Helen or Fiona,
and make me your ravisher!"

In Hospital

1

Naked, and with all
superficialities
reduced to bare life,
as I was born, rolled now to
the adjudicating knife.

2

The perfect crimson
ball of the rising sun burns
through the east window.
After a sleepless night, oh
what relief that the Earth turns.

Reflection

When I consider
those loves and joys untasted,
I don't know whether
I should regret or treasure
the days I may have wasted
watching brown water
slowly bearing drifting leaves
from reflected trees,
down to the creaming weir
where the undercurrent heaves.

In Blantyre Terrace

A blackbird's singing –
clear after summer rain,
filling the Terrace
with sweet nostalgic pain that
siren-songs me home again.

Why are you singing?
Don't you know the difference,
you bird-brain, between
this grey Edinburgh street
and a green Warwickshire lane?

1960 – 1985

From frolic
to colic
in one
generation.

A Kitchen Killing

Some bacteria
got on my dishcloths,
where they multiplied
and set up a stink.
I'm callous, you'll think
without a doubt,
but I determined
to boil the little stinkers out.
Accordingly
– an excess of naked power –
I let them boil for half an hour,
regardless of their
bacterial duty
to live and breed,
and iconoclastic
to bacterial beauty –
a dubious concept,
but to speak bolder,
if beauty is in the eye
of the beholder,
a bacterium
however dutiful
is never beautiful.

At the Giant's Ring

(Co. Down)

Within this giant ring,
older than the fairies,
more grave and more majestic,
there is a place of peace;
not a place of silence
but a place of quiet;
a charmed circle of calm
where the few people's voices,
the cries of children,
and the distant noises
of farm and city
are muted and absorbed
in this tranquillity,
untroubled by the
coloured butterflies,
the grasses and sorrel,
hardheads and thistles
that move continually
in the timeless wind.

And the cromlech at the centre
where sometimes children clamber,
like a skull with little creatures
threading through its empty sockets –
nothing sarcophagal now, but
shelter for the young and harmless,
emanating sanctuary,
especially at evening
when the lights of distant aircraft
can blaze like momentary planets,
portentous, like epiphanies
in the fading dusky light.

Though the earth turns, and darkness falls
over this bank and cloistered ground,
time takes much longer strides here,
moving to a different rhythm

that measures the steps of the slow
couples treading the circle round
and returning on each circuit
to the point of their beginning,
an emblem of eternity;
and the stone slabs at the centre
a benign memento mori.

And many a time,
troubled or distressed,
we have walked here, slowly,
round this circling crest,
with anxious voices, low and tense,
till the motion of our footsteps,
and the passing panorama,
and the calm spirit of this place
have eased the hectic pulse and breath,
anxiety and despair quietly re-focused
into a longer perspective of time;
just as the always drifting wind
strokes and smoothes the bending grasses,
up here, at the Giant's Ring.

Tanka 31

I am the Ice King,
impassive and *comme il faut.*
When you weep like a
distressed child, my snow heart melts,
but my frozen arms can't move.

Pattaya

"Hundreds of bars peddling sex of every variety have made the Thai resort of Pattaya the sleaze capital of Southeast Asia, if not the world . . . estimated 20,000 female prostitutes."
The Observer Colour Supplement, 19th August 1990

Modestly assuming that every whore
is served twice nightly, six nights a week,
(but loses four days work in every month –
though that may be too nice a supposition),
then we may compute, in an average year
seventeen thousand gallons of semen
are voided into the warm vaginas of
the twenty thousand whores of Pattaya.

But if we allow an oral margin,
and a further contribution into
the anal canals of young men and boys,
we may determine that nothing less than
five hundred oil drums brimful of sperm
are the rotting harvest of Pattaya.

The liberal's dilemma

Toleration
tolerated
intolerance,
and so
was not
tolerated.

Elegy IV

At eighty-seven my dreaming mother
forgets that she was ever wife,
that she gave birth. Fragments of life
slip through her fumbling fingers.
Time ebbs, leaving great vacancies –
father, mother, and the long dead
drifting like wraiths through her round head –
waiting, welcoming presences.

It would be pleasant to think so,
that her emptied days might be spent
attended by others who went
before, teaching her how to go.
But I alone am husband, brother
and parent to my orphan mother.

Ghosts

Don't be frightened if you hear us wailing,
lost in the shadow lands of past times,
seeking to walk on remembered floors
in streets that disappeared years ago.
Turn up the radio or whistle a tune
(Oh! to hear an errand-boy whistle a tune!)
And if we should wake you in the night
it is to ask – if we had tongues to utter –
what has become of the nursery?
Why have they taken the Library shelves?
Or where is the little brook that trickled
beside the orchard, which used to grow
where your next-door neighbour's house now stands?
And why do the ash leaves wilt and shrivel?

Tanka 26

A seagull glides by
drowsing afternoon houses,
alien, detached,
past blank reflecting windows,
behind one of which, am I.

Belfast Sunday

Sunday is Hat Day, a day of truce,
unexpected like an overnight
blooming of flowers on a slag-heap,
with a quasi-Ascot elegance
of lacquered style and pastel shades.
Brief quiet falls. The noise of battle stops.
The local generals harangue their troops.

Here Truth is hawked like newspapers,
barked and bawled out on the street corners;
Sunday-pulpit shibboleths blown round
the legs of loafers like litter on the wind.

Truth is devotion that calls us on Sunday
to wear best suits and those formal hats
that are stiff with varnish and Christian virtue.
Never have so many hungry sheep
looked to so many careful pastors
to be fed so very many stones.
Reverend gentlemen howl on their hind legs
resplendent in their sabbath sheepskins;
for theirs is the kingdom, the Power and the Glory.

Truth is a snare-drum that rattles out its rhythm
to the psalming and antheming congregations
and the harsh counterpoint of the shrill fife.
Truth hurls a brickbat at a Peeler;
Truth fires a baton-round at a youngster;
Truth flings a petrol bomb that burns down a house.

Truth here is a lethal weapon
forged on the anvil of history
by the ringing hammer of fear –
reverberations of rhetoric
whose echoes created Ulsterspeak,
that terrible language of Total Conviction.

Graven Images in Fermanagh

Eventually,
at the third attempt,
we found the carved stones.

Whether we were intended to
remains in doubt,
the map inaccurate,
the rain falling faster
and the evening light fading.

Yet, through deliberate persistence
and a dogged intent
we found them.

But what had we found?
Certainly two stone figures,
the smaller weathered past recognition;
but the larger one – or two –
this composite thing
of smooth red sandstone
stood back to back with itself,
a dual entity, a plural thing
with arms (or were they thigh bones?)
crossed in denial – or complacency –
doubling the shape of the closed-V mouth
which leered,
and seemed to jeer and call for drink
both at once, and for ever.

But always, now,
we shall see and feel and hear
that carved silence, that petrified meaning,
perhaps not unconnected with a deep groove
that separated the two heads
at a height convenient
for a stretched neck to rest on.

Having found the stones
there was little else to do
but to photograph them and leave the place,
a dark, damp, ancient graveyard
of small dimensions, sombre, overgrown,
with every headstone broken
like crazy paving scattered in long grass,
except one recent interment;
so that one wondered
how a man could bear
the prospect of lying in such desolation
in a graveyard grove of tall hawthorns and hazel,
dark, dripping with rain.

But that one dead man
beneath the only legible gravestone
I suppose may lie with an ancestral line
native to this secret place,
neither displaced by
nor admingled with
any alien race that has trodden here
since coracles bobbed between the green islands,
and the Great Elk was hunted;
a warrior line
with no sight of time's perspective,
but a long budget of remembered wrongs.

And that line's idol
(if such was ever that stone figure's role)
looks always forward
but yet for ever backward,
the point between them –
unending present –
marked only by that deep groove,
a well-preserved cup
to hold whatever offerings might trickle in,
seep into the stone and,
remarkable to tell,
dissolve not but still harden
the stone heart within.

Elegy V

(*Norrie Masson* d.2000)

We met in my office. He had an appointment –
to remonstrate, I learned, about an oversight –
a justified complaint. I made amends, and then
he mentioned Ireland, I quoted Yeats, and when
we parted (via Coole and Ballylee) we had
charted a course of poetry and prose that would
keep us in close convoy for more than twenty years
until, in words that he himself proposed,
"He went protesting to the grave…"

But, as a man of letters, he understood well
the relative ambivalence of death's full stop,
for he spent a lifetime moving with equal ease
in the dimensions of present space and past time,
yarning with Izaak Walton, exchanging views with Ruskin,
comparing notes with Brahms – a tireless collector
and recorder, and narrator, and connector.
Where he was, strangers spoke and warmed to one another,
woven into the rich pattern of his acquaintance,
themselves enriched by the wide extent of it.
And he extended his lively gift for friendship
to all who welcomed it. I knew no other man
who knew as many interesting people.

But yet, ambivalent though that full stop may be,
in spite of this conceit his death will leave a void
of pain and silence.
But whenever some who knew him come together,
one may remember a *bon mot* he recorded,
someone else a curiosity related
or a tale he told with mischievous delight; and all
will be recalled with laughter, and perhaps a sigh.
So that time, with its grains of recollection,
will seep into the space he has vacated,
fill it up, and gradually harden into
a memorial cast whose form and features
will be defined by those who knew and loved him.

To Rocamadour

1

In late September of my seventieth year
we set out on an easy walking tour
from a sleeping village on the River Dordogne
to the vaguely heard-of town of Rocamadour.
At first we chummed the river, beside and below us,
winding its way through its own civilisation.
But climbing the escarpment
and following the pathways
turned us to the south, and into the gorges,
where all the unnoticed sounds of every day
ceased; and we noticed their ceasing.
And it seemed that Time itself would fall away,
as in a sense it did – its nature changed,
for now its measure was our own walking strides,
and the sun's movement, and the clouds',
and the long, slow arc of the eagle's flight
over the silence of the high limestone cliffs.

And so we came on foot,
trudging the trackways from the great river,
threading the gorges,
gazing upward at the silent cliffs,
counting the eagles – five on the last day –
and entered the town through a narrow gate,
la Porte Basse.
And as we came in under the arch
in broad-brimmed hats and the dust of the tracks,
(no scallop shells, but an old ash plant)
we were incongruous, irrelevant,
as though we had walked in from the Middle Ages.
And as we climbed the steep street
against an indifferent tide of people
flowing down the hill from the cars and coaches
parked at the top of the town,
where the tarmac routes converge and end,
it seemed that we battled up that street.

against the cataract of history –
up that single street from gate to gate,
from la Porte Basse to la Porte du Figuier,
lined with hucksters like villi in an intestine –
those micro-polyps that suck nutrition,
in this case from digested tourists –
just like the old days of pilgrims and plenty.

2
But never so many pilgrims as tourists
you might think,
(though thirty-thousand are said to have camped
in the Alzou valley below the town,
once upon a time).
Saint Bernard and Saint Dominic were both here,
Royal Saint Louis and Philip the Fair.
Henry Plantagenet, restless, violent,
apt to be seized by demonic anger,
found a cure here,
kneeling before la Vierge Noire
like so many other votaries,
the fervid, the desperate, and the quietly ill.
So it is said. And it's probably true.

A long and luminary procession
came to venerate Saint Amadour,
by oral tradition an alias of
little Zaccheus, who climbed a tree
the better to see Jesus pass by;
husband too, of Saint Veronica,
who wiped Christ's face with her veil –
tales of a time when Christianity
was immediate and personal.

Around the saint's remains
was built this city of wonders,
made out of miracles of passionate faith
(but miracles also
of geometry, and of mechanics,)

itself a wonder, if not a miracle,
hanging like a pinnacled swallows' nest
from the limestone overhangs,
out of which it grows.

Here they built a natural machine
whose arcing electrodes of faith and hope
galvanised generations into salvation,
(witness the grooves in the Sanctuary steps –
per ardua ad gloriam on aching knees).

But zeal destroyed what faith had constructed.
The Reformation brought civil war,
and an iconoclast, Captain Bessonies,
who hacked the earthly remains of the saint
into fragments of superstition,
along with the fabrics of shrine and abbey,
empty ruins for two centuries.

3
Returned to Time, the next day,
in crisp-and-cleans like *pukka* tourists,
we entered again,
descending now on the zig-zag path
from the plateau with its overview,
where, in spite of the panorama,
eyes are drawn downward into the gulf
that gouges deeply through the limestone *causse*;
down to where men built this town
on the wall of a gorge.

Its galleried paths and shadowed stairs
lead eventually to the shrine,
where silence in the darkness,
seems to hold its breath,
and Time is not admitted.
The Black Virgin
is an ancient piece of carved wood,
unexpectedly small,

and looms on a shadowed niche,
glimmering in the flicker of the candles.
Each little votive flame is
an intense hope kindled into tiny fire,
wavering, but unextinguished by the draught.
Each yellow flame is a source of light and heat
in the cold darkness of the living rock.

4

Meanwhile outside in the warm air
the brilliant sun
accentuates the starkness of the cut stone
against the deep blue glow of the sky.

But while the body absorbs this unaccustomed balm,
a thought lingers in the dark shrine
and will not come away.
Persistently an endless flow of past folk
nameless, long dead, and unremembered save
for the negative imprints of the hollowed steps,
shuffles upward and upward to that inmost dark
in which so many hoped to find an inward light.

And those who found a light –
and those who found a cure –
was it indeed their faith that made them whole?
Had they carried with them
all the time, but unawares,
that which they had sought?
Does faith (or whatever it is that does the trick)
need some kind of process,
a trigger, to release its fullest power
as winter wheat needs to feel the frost
before it can fruit?
And is it the journey or the destination –
the key that unlocks that secret inner door
through which they hoped to pass?

5

And now, up here at Latitude 56,
where Moscow is our nearest parallel city,
and the small, pale, clouded sun
seems no more than a distant cousin
of the great Jovial beamer
that ruled the sky over Rocamadour,
I reflect that my allotted span
of three score years and ten is spent;
that what is left will be played in Extra Time;
and it seems like the end of a chapter,
if not quite the end of the book.
But perhaps there may be an epilogue,
for there is this at least –
Our walking tour was a lifetime's first; and yet
the further we walked, the less it seemed like a journey
and the more it seemed to become a destination,
like a rite of passage or a crossing point.

Fresh from the shrine, I had mused upon
what the pilgrims had taken with them.
Now I ponder on what it is that they – and we,
unwitting pilgrims that we found ourselves to be –
brought away from that strange cliff-hanging little town
that was founded on faith and the literal
expectation of resurrection.

To my own book I expect no sequel,
but in the Finale, look for a twist in the plot.